Factors Shaping Sexual Attraction in Children: A Parent's Perspective

Table of Contents

Factors Shaping Sexual Attraction in Children: A Parent's Perspective

By Roberto Miguel Rodriguez

Chapter 1: Introduction

Understanding the Importance of Sexual Attraction Development in Children

Sexual attraction development in children is a critical and complex aspect of their overall growth and development. As parents and educators, it is crucial for us to comprehend the factors that shape and influence this development to ensure the healthy and appropriate progression of their understanding of sexuality.

Factors influencing the development of sexual attraction in children are multifaceted and include both internal and external elements. Biological and neurological factors, such as hormonal changes, play a significant role in the onset of sexual attraction. Understanding these mechanisms can help parents and educators navigate this period of development with sensitivity and knowledge.

The role of media and technology in shaping sexual attraction in children cannot be underestimated. Exposure to explicit content at an early age can distort their understanding of healthy relationships and sexuality. It is essential for parents and educators to monitor and limit their exposure to age-appropriate content, fostering open and honest discussions to counteract any negative influences.

Cultural influences also have a profound impact on the development of sexual attraction in children. Society's norms, values, and expectations can shape their understanding of gender roles, body image, and sexual orientation. Encouraging diversity, inclusivity, and open-mindedness can help children develop a healthy and accepting attitude towards others' sexual attractions.

Parental guidance plays a crucial role in the development of sexual attraction in children. Providing accurate and age-appropriate information, fostering open communication, and promoting positive body image and self-esteem can positively shape their understanding of sexuality. Parents should create a safe and non-judgmental environment for children to ask questions and seek guidance.

Peer influence also plays a significant role in the development of sexual attraction in children. Friends and classmates can expose children to new ideas, behaviors, and norms. Educators and parents need to encourage healthy friendships and provide guidance on navigating peer pressure to prevent the development of inappropriate sexual attractions.

Psychological and emotional factors can influence the development of sexual attraction in children. Traumatic experiences or emotional instability can impact their understanding of healthy relationships. Addressing and providing support for these underlying issues is crucial to promoting healthy sexual attraction development.

Education and awareness programs are vital for fostering healthy sexual attraction development in children. These programs should provide age-appropriate information, promote consent, and teach children about healthy relationships. Parents and educators should actively seek out and support such programs in schools and communities.

Early childhood experiences can have a lasting impact on the development of sexual attraction. Providing a safe and nurturing environment, free from abuse or trauma, is vital for healthy development. Early intervention and support for children who have experienced adverse experiences can help mitigate any negative effects on their understanding of sexuality.

Neurological and hormonal factors, such as puberty, can significantly affect the development of sexual attraction in children. Understanding these biological changes can help parents and educators provide appropriate guidance and support during this transformative period.

In cases where inappropriate sexual attraction arises in children, intervention strategies should be implemented promptly. Seeking professional help from therapists or psychologists can assist in addressing and redirecting these behaviors, ensuring the child's healthy sexual development.

Understanding the importance of sexual attraction development in children is paramount for parents and educators. By comprehending the factors that shape and influence this development, we can provide the necessary guidance, support, and education to ensure children develop a healthy and positive understanding of their own sexuality and that of others.

The Role of Parents and Educators in Nurturing Healthy Sexual Attraction

In today's society, understanding the factors shaping sexual attraction in children is essential for parents and educators. As children go through various stages of development, their understanding of sexual attraction begins to form. It is crucial for parents and educators to play an active role in nurturing healthy sexual attraction in children.

Factors influencing the development of sexual attraction in children are numerous and complex. The media and technology have a significant impact on shaping children's understanding of sexuality. From explicit content to unrealistic portrayals of relationships, children are exposed to a wide range of influences that can shape their perception of sexual attraction. Parents and educators must be aware of the media their children are consuming and provide guidance and context to help them navigate these influences.

Cultural influences also play a vital role in the development of sexual attraction in children. Different cultures have different norms and values when it comes to sexuality. Parents and educators need to be sensitive to these cultural differences and provide age-appropriate information and guidance that aligns with their cultural beliefs.

Parental guidance is one of the most influential factors in shaping healthy sexual attraction in children. Open and honest communication about sexuality is essential. Parents should create a safe and supportive environment where children feel comfortable asking questions and discussing their feelings. Providing accurate information at an age-appropriate level is crucial to help children develop a healthy understanding of sexual attraction.

Peer influence also plays a significant role in shaping sexual attraction in children. Peers can influence their attitudes, behaviors, and beliefs about sexuality. Parents and educators should encourage positive peer relationships and provide guidance on healthy boundaries and respectful behavior.

Psychological and emotional factors can also influence sexual attraction in children. Traumatic experiences or a lack of emotional support can impact how children develop their understanding of sexuality. It is crucial for parents and educators to create an emotionally nurturing environment that supports a healthy development of sexual attraction.

Education and awareness programs are valuable tools for parents and educators. These programs can provide accurate information, dispel myths, and promote healthy attitudes towards sexuality. By incorporating comprehensive sexuality education into school curricula, children can develop a well-rounded understanding of sexual attraction.

Early childhood experiences can have a lasting impact on the development of sexual attraction. It is important for parents and educators to provide a nurturing and supportive environment during these formative years. This includes promoting healthy relationships, teaching consent, and providing age-appropriate information about bodies and boundaries.

Neurological and hormonal factors also affect the development of sexual attraction in children. Understanding these biological influences can help parents and educators approach the topic of sexuality with empathy and compassion.

In cases where inappropriate sexual attraction arises, intervention strategies are crucial. Promptly addressing these issues with professional guidance can help prevent further harm and ensure the child receives the support they need.

In conclusion, parents and educators play a vital role in nurturing healthy sexual attraction in children. By understanding the factors shaping sexual attraction and being proactive in providing guidance, parents and educators can create a safe and supportive environment for children to develop a healthy understanding of sexuality.

Overview of the Book's Structure and Objectives

Understanding the Factors Shaping Sexual Attraction in Children: A Parent's Perspective is a comprehensive guide that aims to provide parents and educators with valuable insights into the development of sexual attraction in children. This book delves into various factors that influence the development of sexual attraction, including media and technology, cultural influences, parental guidance, peer influence, psychological and emotional factors, education and awareness programs, early childhood experiences, neurological and hormonal factors, and intervention strategies for addressing inappropriate sexual attraction.

The book is structured in a logical and organized manner, with each chapter focusing on a specific aspect of the development of sexual attraction in children. The chapters are designed to provide a deep understanding of the topic, ensuring that parents and educators are well-equipped to navigate this sensitive area with confidence and knowledge.

The first few chapters lay the foundation by introducing the concept of sexual attraction in children and examining the various factors that contribute to its development. The role of media and technology in shaping sexual attraction is explored, highlighting the need for vigilance and guidance in the digital age. Cultural influences on sexual attraction are also discussed, emphasizing the importance of recognizing and respecting diverse cultural perspectives.

The subsequent chapters delve into the crucial role of parental guidance in shaping healthy sexual attraction in children. Strategies for open communication, setting boundaries, and providing age-appropriate information are explored, enabling parents to establish a supportive and nurturing environment.

Peer influence is another significant aspect addressed in this book. The impact of friendships, social dynamics, and peer pressure on the development of sexual attraction is thoroughly examined, equipping parents and educators with strategies to mitigate any negative influences.

Furthermore, the book explores the psychological and emotional factors that can influence sexual attraction in children, emphasizing the need for a holistic approach to their well-being. Education and awareness programs are also highlighted as effective tools for promoting healthy sexual attraction development.

The book also delves into the impact of early childhood experiences on the development of sexual attraction, shedding light on the importance of a nurturing and secure environment during the formative years. Additionally, the role of neurological and hormonal factors is explored, providing a comprehensive understanding of the biological aspects of sexual attraction.

Finally, the book concludes with a chapter on intervention strategies for addressing inappropriate sexual attraction in children. Proactive measures, such as early detection, professional guidance, and therapeutic interventions, are discussed, enabling parents and educators to effectively support children facing such challenges.

In summary, Understanding the Factors Shaping Sexual Attraction in Children: A Parent's Perspective is a valuable resource for parents and educators seeking to navigate the complex topic of sexual attraction in children. By providing a comprehensive overview of various factors influencing its development and offering practical strategies for promoting healthy sexual attraction, this book empowers readers to foster a safe and supportive environment for children's emotional and psychological well-being.

Chapter 2: The Development of Sexual Attraction in Children

Exploring the Natural Progression of Sexual Attraction in Childhood

Understanding the development of sexual attraction in children is crucial for parents and educators to create a safe and supportive environment for their children. This subchapter delves into the natural progression of sexual attraction in childhood, examining various factors that influence its development and exploring strategies for addressing inappropriate sexual attraction.

The development of sexual attraction in children is a complex process influenced by numerous factors. One key factor to consider is the role of media and technology. In today's digital age, children are exposed to explicit content at an earlier age, which can impact their understanding of sexuality. Parents and educators must be vigilant in monitoring their children's media consumption and promoting age-appropriate content.

Cultural influences also shape a child's understanding of sexual attraction. Different cultures have varying attitudes towards sexuality, and these beliefs can impact a child's development. It is essential for parents and educators to engage in open and honest discussions about cultural norms and values surrounding sexuality, while also emphasizing the importance of respect and consent.

Parental guidance plays a critical role in shaping a child's understanding of sexual attraction. Parents must provide accurate and age-appropriate information, while also creating a safe space for their children to ask questions and express their feelings. By establishing open lines of communication, parents can help their children navigate the complexities of sexual attraction in a healthy and informed manner.

Peer influence is another significant factor in the development of sexual attraction. As children grow older, they may rely more on their peers for information and validation. Educators can play a vital role in promoting positive peer relationships and providing guidance on healthy boundaries and consent.

Psychological and emotional factors also influence sexual attraction in children. Factors such as self-esteem, body image, and emotional well-being can impact a child's understanding and expression of their own sexuality. It is essential for parents and educators to foster a positive self-image and provide resources for emotional support when needed.

Education and awareness programs are crucial for promoting healthy sexual attraction development in children. Schools and communities should implement comprehensive sex education programs that emphasize consent, healthy relationships, and understanding boundaries. By providing accurate information in a safe and supportive environment, educators can empower children to make informed decisions about their own sexuality.

Early childhood experiences, including trauma or abuse, can impact the development of sexual attraction. It is vital for parents and educators to be aware of the potential effects of early experiences and seek professional help if necessary. By addressing and resolving any underlying issues, children can develop a healthier understanding of sexual attraction.

Neurological and hormonal factors also play a role in the development of sexual attraction. As children go through puberty, their bodies undergo significant changes that can influence their feelings and attractions. Understanding these biological factors can help parents and educators provide appropriate support and guidance during this crucial stage of development.

Finally, intervention strategies are essential for addressing inappropriate sexual attraction in children. If a child exhibits concerning behaviors or displays a lack of understanding about appropriate boundaries, it is crucial to seek professional help. Intervention strategies may include therapy, counseling, or support groups to address and redirect inappropriate behavior.

In conclusion, understanding the natural progression of sexual attraction in childhood is essential for parents and educators. By exploring the various factors that influence its development, such as media, culture, parental guidance, peer influence, and psychological factors, we can create an environment that fosters healthy sexual attraction development in children. By implementing education and awareness programs, addressing early childhood experiences, considering neurological and hormonal factors, and utilizing intervention strategies when necessary, we can provide the support and guidance children need to navigate their sexuality in a safe and respectful manner.

Age-Appropriate Sexual Development Milestones

Understanding the Factors Shaping Sexual Attraction in Children: A Parent's Perspective

Chapter X: Age-Appropriate Sexual Development Milestones

As parents and educators, it is crucial to understand the developmental milestones that children go through in terms of their sexual attraction. By recognizing these milestones, we can better support our children and provide them with appropriate guidance as they navigate this aspect of their lives. In this subchapter, we will explore the age-appropriate sexual development milestones that children commonly experience.

1. Early Childhood (Ages 0-5):

During this stage, children develop a basic understanding of their own bodies and differences between genders. They may exhibit curiosity about their genitals and engage in age-appropriate exploration. Parents can provide guidance by using correct terminology, promoting body autonomy, and teaching boundaries with others.

2. Middle Childhood (Ages 6-12):

At this stage, children become more aware of societal norms and expectations regarding gender roles. They may develop innocent crushes and engage in non-sexualized romantic play. It is important for parents and educators to encourage open communication, answer questions honestly, and promote healthy relationships based on respect and consent.

3. Adolescence (Ages 13-18):

During adolescence, hormonal changes and the onset of puberty significantly impact sexual development. Adolescents may experience sexual attraction and engage in more romantic relationships. It is crucial for parents and educators to address topics such as consent, safe sex, and healthy relationships. Open dialogue and non-judgmental support are vital during this stage.

It is important to note that these milestones serve as general guidelines, and every child develops at their own pace. Factors such as cultural influences, media exposure, and individual experiences can also shape a child's sexual development. Therefore, it is essential for parents and educators to be mindful of these influences and provide appropriate guidance and support.

In the next subchapters, we will delve deeper into the factors influencing the development of sexual attraction in children, including the role of media and technology, cultural influences, parental guidance, peer influence, psychological and emotional factors, and the impact of early childhood experiences. We will also explore education and awareness programs that promote healthy sexual attraction development and intervention strategies for addressing inappropriate sexual attraction in children.

By understanding these factors and milestones, parents and educators can play a crucial role in fostering healthy sexual development in children, ensuring their overall well-being and safety.

Common Misconceptions and Myths about Childhood Sexual Attraction

When it comes to the development of sexual attraction in children, there are several misconceptions and myths that circulate among parents and educators. It is crucial to debunk these misconceptions and myths to ensure that we have a better understanding of this complex topic and can provide appropriate guidance to children. In this subchapter, we will address some of the most common misconceptions and myths about childhood sexual attraction.

One common misconception is that children do not experience sexual attraction at all. This is simply not true. Research has shown that children do indeed experience sexual attraction, although it may manifest differently than in adults. It is essential for parents and educators to acknowledge and address this reality in a healthy and age-appropriate manner.

Another myth is that exposure to media and technology is the primary factor influencing the development of sexual attraction in children. While media and technology play a role, they are just one piece of the puzzle. Factors such as biological, psychological, and emotional influences also contribute to the development of sexual attraction in children. It is important not to solely blame media and technology without considering the broader context.

Cultural influences on the development of sexual attraction are often overlooked. Each culture has its own norms and values regarding sexuality, and children are influenced by these cultural messages. It is crucial for parents and educators to recognize and address these cultural influences to ensure a healthy understanding of sexual attraction.

Another misconception is that parental guidance alone can determine the development of sexual attraction in children. While parental guidance is undeniably important, it is not the sole determining factor. Peer influence, early childhood experiences, neurological and hormonal factors, and education also play crucial roles. It is necessary to consider a holistic approach that takes into account all these factors.

Furthermore, it is essential to debunk the myth that inappropriate sexual attraction in children is solely a result of external influences. While external factors can contribute, there are often underlying psychological and emotional factors that need to be addressed.

Intervention strategies should focus on understanding and addressing these underlying factors rather than solely blaming external influences.

In conclusion, understanding the factors shaping sexual attraction in children requires debunking common misconceptions and myths. By addressing these misconceptions and myths, parents and educators can gain a more accurate understanding of childhood sexual attraction and provide appropriate guidance to children. It is crucial to consider all the factors influencing the development of sexual attraction and to approach the topic holistically.

Chapter 3: Factors Influencing the Development of Sexual Attraction in Children

Genetic and Biological Factors

Understanding the Factors Shaping Sexual Attraction in Children: A Parent's Perspective

As parents and educators, it is crucial for us to gain a comprehensive understanding of the factors that shape sexual attraction in children. One significant aspect to consider is the role of genetic and biological factors in this complex process.

Research indicates that genetic factors play a role in the development of sexual attraction. Studies have shown that certain genes may influence the timing and intensity of sexual maturation in children. For example, variations in genes related to hormone production and receptor sensitivity can impact the onset of puberty, which in turn may influence sexual attraction. While genetics does play a role, it is important to note that it is not the sole determining factor.

Biological factors, such as hormonal changes, also contribute to the development of sexual attraction. During puberty, there is an increase in sex hormone production, which can influence a child's sexual thoughts and desires. The interplay between hormones and brain development during this critical period can shape sexual attraction patterns.

It is essential for parents and educators to recognize that while genetic and biological factors lay the foundation, they do not solely determine a child's sexual attraction. Environmental factors, such as media and technology, cultural influences, parental guidance, and peer interactions, also play significant roles.

Understanding the impact of genetic and biological factors can help parents and educators navigate discussions and provide appropriate guidance. It is crucial to create an open and honest dialogue with children about their changing bodies and emerging feelings. By providing accurate information and addressing any concerns, parents and educators can help children navigate their developing sexual attraction in a healthy and safe manner.

Furthermore, education and awareness programs can be implemented to promote healthy sexual attraction development in children. These programs can help children understand their emotions, foster respectful relationships, and provide them with the tools to make informed decisions.

In cases where inappropriate sexual attraction arises, intervention strategies should be implemented. These strategies may involve seeking professional help, creating a supportive environment, and teaching appropriate boundaries.

In conclusion, genetic and biological factors are foundational in the development of sexual attraction in children. However, it is crucial to recognize the influence of environmental factors, such as media, culture, and parental guidance. By understanding these factors, parents and educators can play a pivotal role in promoting healthy sexual attraction development and addressing any challenges that may arise.

Environmental Influences

Environmental influences play a significant role in shaping the development of sexual attraction in children. As parents and educators, it is crucial to understand these factors and their impact on children's perception of sexuality. This subchapter aims to provide insight into the various environmental influences that contribute to the formation of sexual attraction in children and offer guidance on how to navigate these influences effectively.

One of the most prominent factors influencing the development of sexual attraction in children is the role of media and technology. Today's children are exposed to a wide array of media content, including television shows, movies, music videos, and internet platforms. These media sources often depict relationships and sexuality in an unrealistic and distorted manner, leading to misconceptions and inappropriate expectations. It is essential for parents and educators to monitor and regulate children's exposure to media content, encouraging healthy discussions, and providing accurate information.

Cultural influences also play a significant role in shaping children's perception of sexual attraction. Different cultures have varying attitudes, values, and beliefs regarding sexuality. Parents and educators must be aware of these cultural influences and engage in open and non-judgmental conversations with children about their sexuality. By fostering an inclusive and accepting environment, children can develop a healthy understanding of their own sexual attraction and respect for others.

Parental guidance is another crucial factor in the development of sexual attraction in children. Parents should provide age-appropriate information about sexuality and establish an open line of communication. By addressing their children's questions and concerns in a supportive manner, parents can help children navigate the complexities of sexual attraction and develop a healthy self-image.

Peer influence also plays a significant role in the development of sexual attraction in children. As children grow older, they often seek validation and approval from their peers. It is crucial for parents and educators to guide children in choosing healthy friendships and understanding the impact of peer influence on their perception of sexuality.

Psychological and emotional factors, such as self-esteem, body image, and past experiences, can significantly influence children's sexual attraction. Parents and educators should be mindful of these factors and provide appropriate support and resources to help children develop a positive self-image and healthy relationships.

Education and awareness programs are essential for promoting healthy sexual attraction development in children. Schools and communities should implement age-appropriate and evidence-based sexual education programs that address consent, healthy relationships, and respect for diversity.

Early childhood experiences, including attachment patterns and exposure to trauma, can also impact the development of sexual attraction in children. It is crucial for parents and educators to be sensitive to these experiences and provide appropriate support and intervention when necessary.

Neurological and hormonal factors also contribute to the development of sexual attraction in children. Understanding these biological processes can help parents and educators navigate discussions around sexuality and address any concerns or questions that may arise.

Lastly, intervention strategies are necessary for addressing inappropriate sexual attraction in children. It is essential to approach these situations with empathy and seek professional help when needed. By providing a safe and supportive environment, children can receive the necessary guidance and resources to navigate their sexual attraction appropriately.

In conclusion, understanding the various environmental influences on the development of sexual attraction in children is crucial for parents and educators. By being aware of these factors and engaging in open and supportive conversations, we can help children develop a healthy understanding of their sexuality and navigate the complexities of sexual attraction.

Family Dynamics and Parental Relationships

The development of sexual attraction in children is a complex process influenced by various factors, including family dynamics and parental relationships. Parents and educators play a crucial role in understanding and shaping this aspect of their child's life. This subchapter will explore the importance of family dynamics and parental relationships in relation to the development of sexual attraction in children.

Family dynamics have a significant impact on a child's understanding of relationships and their own self-identity. When children are exposed to healthy, loving, and respectful relationships within their family, they are more likely to develop positive attitudes towards intimacy and healthy sexual attraction. On the other hand, children who witness conflict, violence, or dysfunctional relationships may struggle with their own relationships and exhibit inappropriate sexual attraction.

Parental relationships also influence the development of sexual attraction in children. Children observe and learn from their parents' interactions, including how they communicate, handle conflicts, and express love and affection. When parents model healthy relationships, children are more likely to form healthy attachments and develop appropriate sexual attraction. Conversely, if parents display unhealthy behaviors or lack emotional connection, it can impact their child's understanding of relationships and sexual attraction.

Media and technology play an increasingly significant role in shaping children's understanding of sexuality. Parents and educators need to be aware of the impact of media on their child's development and provide guidance accordingly. Monitoring media exposure, discussing age-appropriate content, and promoting critical thinking skills can help children navigate the messages they receive and develop a healthy understanding of sexual attraction.

Cultural influences also play a crucial role in the development of sexual attraction in children. Different cultures have different norms and values related to sexuality, and children may internalize these beliefs. It is essential for parents and educators to understand and respect cultural diversity while providing accurate information and fostering open discussions about sexual attraction.

Parental guidance is vital in shaping healthy sexual attraction in children. Open communication, providing accurate information, and creating a safe environment for discussions can help children develop a positive attitude towards their bodies, relationships, and sexuality. Parents should be prepared to answer questions, address concerns, and provide age-appropriate education about sexual attraction.

Peer influence is another significant factor in the development of sexual attraction in children. As children grow older, their peers become more influential in shaping their attitudes and behaviors. Parents and educators need to encourage healthy peer relationships and provide guidance on establishing boundaries and making informed choices.

Psychological and emotional factors also influence sexual attraction in children. Factors such as self-esteem, body image, and emotional well-being can impact how children perceive themselves and others. Parents and educators should promote positive self-image, emotional intelligence, and healthy coping mechanisms to support healthy sexual attraction development.

Education and awareness programs are essential for promoting healthy sexual attraction development in children. Schools and parents should collaborate to provide comprehensive sex education that focuses on consent, healthy relationships, and respect. These programs should be age-appropriate, inclusive, and free from stigma or shame.

Early childhood experiences, such as attachment styles and caregiver interactions, can shape a child's understanding of relationships and intimacy. Positive early experiences can foster healthy emotional development and lay the foundation for healthy sexual attraction later in life.

Neurological and hormonal factors also play a role in the development of sexual attraction in children. Understanding these biological processes can help parents and educators recognize normal development and identify potential issues that require professional intervention.

Finally, intervention strategies are necessary for addressing inappropriate sexual attraction in children. It is essential for parents and educators to be vigilant, recognize signs of inappropriate behavior, and seek professional help when needed. Early intervention can prevent further harm and support the child's healthy development.

In conclusion, family dynamics and parental relationships significantly influence the development of sexual attraction in children. Parents and educators have a critical role in understanding and shaping this aspect of their child's life. By fostering healthy relationships, providing accurate information, promoting open communication, and seeking professional help when needed, they can support children in developing a healthy understanding of sexual attraction.

Sibling Relationships and Birth Order Effects

Sibling relationships and birth order have a significant impact on the development of sexual attraction in children. Understanding this dynamic is essential for parents and educators to provide appropriate guidance and support to children as they navigate their feelings and emotions.

Research has shown that sibling relationships play a crucial role in shaping a child's understanding of relationships, intimacy, and attraction. Siblings serve as early models for social interactions, teaching children how to communicate, share, and develop emotional connections. These early experiences can influence a child's later romantic relationships and sexual attraction.

Birth order also plays a role in the development of sexual attraction. First-born children, for example, often exhibit traits associated with leadership, responsibility, and assertiveness. These characteristics may influence their approach to relationships and attraction. In contrast, younger siblings may develop different traits, such as being more nurturing or seeking attention, which can shape their own patterns of attraction.

Media and technology also have a profound impact on children's understanding of sexual attraction. The prevalence of explicit content and easy access to pornography can distort a child's perception of healthy relationships and influence their sexual desires. Parents and educators must be vigilant in monitoring children's media consumption and providing age-appropriate education to counteract these negative influences.

Cultural influences further shape children's understanding of sexual attraction. Norms, values, and beliefs regarding relationships and sexuality vary across cultures, and children internalize these messages from an early age. It is crucial for parents and educators to provide a safe and inclusive environment where children can explore their feelings and ask questions without judgment.

Parental guidance is of utmost importance in shaping a child's understanding of sexual attraction. Open and honest communication about relationships, consent, and boundaries is essential. Parents should also be aware of their own attitudes and beliefs about sexuality and ensure they are providing accurate information and fostering a positive attitude towards healthy relationships.

Peer influence is another factor that affects the development of sexual attraction. Children often look to their peers for validation and acceptance, which can influence their own feelings and desires. Educators can play a pivotal role in promoting healthy peer relationships and providing guidance on navigating attraction and relationships.

Psychological and emotional factors, such as self-esteem, body image, and attachment styles, also influence a child's development of sexual attraction. Children with positive self-esteem and a healthy body image are more likely to navigate relationships in a healthier and more positive way.

Education and awareness programs are vital in promoting healthy sexual attraction development in children. These programs should focus on teaching children about consent, boundaries, and healthy relationships. They should also address issues of gender equality, diversity, and inclusion.

Early childhood experiences, including attachment patterns and exposure to trauma, can shape a child's development of sexual attraction. It is essential for parents and educators to create a nurturing and supportive environment that promotes healthy attachment and addresses any potential traumatic experiences.

Neurological and hormonal factors also influence the development of sexual attraction. Understanding the biological aspects of attraction can help parents and educators better support children in navigating their feelings and emotions.

Lastly, intervention strategies are necessary for addressing inappropriate sexual attraction in children. Early identification and intervention can prevent harmful behaviors and promote healthy development. Parents and educators should be knowledgeable about available resources and seek professional help when needed.

In conclusion, understanding the factors shaping sexual attraction in children is crucial for parents and educators. Sibling relationships, birth order effects, media influence, cultural norms, parental guidance, peer influence, psychological and emotional factors, education programs, early childhood experiences, neurological and hormonal factors, and intervention strategies all play a significant role in the development of sexual attraction in children. By being aware of these factors and providing appropriate guidance and support, parents and educators can help children navigate their feelings and emotions in a healthy and positive way.

Chapter 4: The Role of Media and Technology in Shaping Sexual Attraction in Children

Media Exposure and Its Impact on Sexual Attraction Development

In today's digital age, media and technology play a significant role in shaping the development of sexual attraction in children. As parents and educators, it is crucial to understand the influence of media exposure on our children and how it impacts their understanding and perception of sexual attraction.

The media, including television shows, movies, music videos, and social media platforms, bombards children with various images and messages related to sexuality. These constant exposures can shape their beliefs, attitudes, and behaviors towards sexual attraction. Research suggests that media exposure can lead to early sexualization, the objectification of oneself and others, and the normalization of unhealthy sexual behaviors.

Factors such as the portrayal of unrealistic body ideals, explicit sexual content, and the glamorization of casual sex contribute to the shaping of children's sexual attraction. Studies have shown that children who are exposed to sexual content at an early age are more likely to engage in risky sexual behaviors during adolescence. It is therefore crucial for parents and educators to monitor and regulate media consumption to protect children from harmful influences.

Cultural influences also play a significant role in shaping children's sexual attraction. Different cultures have varying norms and values regarding sexuality, and media often reinforces these cultural beliefs. For example, in some cultures, modesty and abstinence before marriage are highly valued, while in others, sexual liberation is encouraged.

Parents and educators must be aware of these cultural influences and engage in open and honest conversations with children to provide them with a comprehensive understanding of sexual attraction that aligns with their values.

Parental guidance is paramount in mitigating the negative impact of media exposure on sexual attraction development. Parents should actively engage in conversations about sexuality, provide accurate information, and establish clear boundaries regarding media consumption. By fostering a healthy and open environment, parents can help their children develop a positive and respectful understanding of sexual attraction.

In addition to parental guidance, peer influence also plays a significant role in shaping children's sexual attraction. Peers often share media content among themselves, and the influence of friends can impact children's attitudes and behaviors towards sexual attraction. Educators can play a vital role in promoting healthy sexual attraction development by incorporating comprehensive sex education programs that address the influence of media and peer pressure.

Psychological and emotional factors also influence the development of sexual attraction in children. Traumatic experiences, such as abuse or neglect, can significantly impact a child's understanding and perception of sexual attraction. It is crucial for parents and educators to recognize these factors and provide appropriate support and intervention to address any inappropriate sexual attraction.

Education and awareness programs focused on healthy sexual attraction development are essential in equipping children with the necessary knowledge and skills to navigate their sexuality. These programs should address consent, healthy relationships, and the influence of media, among other relevant topics. By providing comprehensive education and fostering open dialogue, parents and educators can empower children to make informed and responsible choices regarding their sexual attraction.

Early childhood experiences, including attachment, bonding, and caregiver interactions, have a profound impact on the development of sexual attraction. Positive and nurturing early experiences can help children develop a healthy sense of self and establish secure relationships, which in turn positively influence their understanding and expression of sexual attraction.

Neurological and hormonal factors also contribute to the development of sexual attraction in children. Research suggests that brain development and hormonal changes during puberty influence the awakening of sexual feelings and attractions. Parents and educators should be aware of these physiological changes and provide appropriate support and guidance to help children navigate this phase of development.

In cases where inappropriate sexual attraction arises, intervention strategies are crucial. It is essential for parents and educators to address these issues promptly and seek professional help if necessary. Open communication, counseling, and therapy can play a significant role in understanding the underlying causes and providing appropriate support to children.

In conclusion, media exposure has a profound impact on the development of sexual attraction in children. Parents and educators must be proactive in understanding and addressing the influence of media on children's understanding and perception of sexual attraction. By providing guidance, fostering open dialogue, and promoting comprehensive education, we can empower children to develop healthy and respectful attitudes towards their sexual attraction.

Internet and Social Media Influence on Children's Understanding of Attraction

In today's digital age, the internet and social media have become an integral part of children's lives. They provide a wealth of information, opportunities for communication, and exposure to various perspectives. However, it is important for parents and educators to understand the potential influence of these platforms on children's understanding of attraction, particularly in the context of their sexual development.

The internet and social media offer children access to a wide range of content, including explicit material and unrealistic portrayals of relationships. This exposure can shape their perceptions of attraction and intimacy, leading to distorted expectations and confusion about healthy relationships. It is crucial for parents and educators to be aware of the content their children are consuming and to engage in open conversations about these topics.

Additionally, the internet and social media can contribute to the normalization of certain behaviors or attitudes related to attraction. For example, online platforms may perpetuate harmful stereotypes or objectify individuals based on their physical appearance. This can influence children's understanding of what is considered attractive and lead to unrealistic standards.

Moreover, social media platforms often emphasize external validation through likes, comments, and followers. This can create a sense of pressure for children to conform to societal beauty standards and seek validation based on their physical appearance. It is essential for parents and educators to help children develop a healthy sense of self-worth that is not solely dependent on external validation.

Furthermore, the internet and social media can expose children to online predators or inappropriate content, which may negatively impact their understanding of attraction and boundaries. It is crucial for parents and educators to monitor their children's online activities, set clear boundaries, and educate them about online safety.

To mitigate the negative impact of internet and social media on children's understanding of attraction, parents and educators must play an active role. This includes fostering open and honest communication, providing age-appropriate education about healthy relationships and boundaries, and setting guidelines for internet and social media use.

In conclusion, the internet and social media have a significant influence on children's understanding of attraction. Parents and educators must be proactive in guiding children's online experiences, promoting healthy relationship dynamics, and addressing any misconceptions or unhealthy behaviors that may arise. By understanding the factors shaping sexual attraction in children and actively engaging in their development, we can help them navigate the digital landscape and foster healthy attitudes towards attraction and relationships.

Strategies for Monitoring and Limiting Media Influence

In today's digital age, media plays a significant role in shaping the development of sexual attraction in children. As parents and educators, it is crucial to understand the influence of media and technology and implement effective strategies to monitor and limit its impact on children. By doing so, we can ensure that children develop a healthy understanding of sexuality and make informed decisions.

One of the first strategies to consider is setting clear boundaries and guidelines for media consumption. Establish age-appropriate restrictions on the types of media content children can access. Regularly monitor their online activities and explain the reasons behind the limitations. Encourage open communication so that children feel comfortable discussing any concerns or questions they may have about the media they encounter.

Another strategy is to actively engage with the media children consume. Watch movies, TV shows, and online content together as a family. This allows you to assess the appropriateness of the content and enables you to discuss any confusing or inappropriate messages portrayed. Use these opportunities to teach critical thinking skills and help children analyze the media's influence on their perception of sexual attraction.

Cultural influences also play a significant role in shaping children's understanding of sexuality. As parents and educators, it is important to expose children to diverse cultural perspectives on sexuality. This can be achieved through literature, movies, and discussions about different cultural norms and values. By providing a broader context, children can develop a more nuanced understanding of sexual attraction and diversity.

Parental guidance and education are vital in mitigating the negative effects of media on children's sexual attraction development. Stay informed about the latest media trends and technologies to better understand their potential impact. Educate yourself about healthy sexual development and be prepared to have open and honest conversations with your children. Provide accurate and age-appropriate information to address any misconceptions or misinformation they may encounter.

Lastly, be mindful of peer influence. Encourage children to form healthy friendships and surround themselves with positive role models. Foster an environment where children feel comfortable discussing their experiences and concerns with their peers, while also promoting respect and consent.

In conclusion, monitoring and limiting media influence on the development of sexual attraction in children requires proactive strategies and open communication. By setting boundaries, actively engaging with media, considering cultural influences, providing parental guidance, and addressing peer influence, parents and educators can help children navigate the complex world of media and develop a healthy understanding of sexual attraction.

Chapter 5: Cultural Influences on the Development of Sexual Attraction in Children

Cultural Variations in Attitudes towards Sexuality

Understanding the Factors Shaping Sexual Attraction in Children: A Parent's Perspective

Parents and educators play a crucial role in guiding children as they navigate the complex and ever-changing world of sexuality. One important aspect to consider is the cultural variations in attitudes towards sexuality that can significantly influence a child's development of sexual attraction. It is essential to recognize and understand these cultural influences to provide appropriate guidance and support to children.

Cultural influences on the development of sexual attraction in children can vary greatly across different societies and communities. Some cultures may have more conservative attitudes, viewing sexuality as a taboo subject that should not be openly discussed. In contrast, other cultures may have more liberal views, promoting open discussions about sexuality from an early age. These cultural variations can impact how children perceive and understand their own sexual feelings and attraction.

The role of media and technology in shaping sexual attraction in children is another crucial factor to consider. In today's digital age, children are exposed to a wide range of media content that can influence their attitudes towards sexuality. Pornography, explicit music videos, and social media platforms can provide unrealistic and often harmful portrayals of sexual relationships. Parents and educators must be vigilant in monitoring and guiding children's media consumption to ensure they receive accurate and age-appropriate information about sexuality.

Parental guidance and its impact on the development of sexual attraction in children cannot be overstated. Parents play a central role in shaping their children's attitudes and beliefs about sexuality. Open and honest communication between parents and children is essential for fostering a healthy understanding of sexuality. Parents should create a safe and non-judgmental environment where children feel comfortable discussing their questions and concerns about sexual attraction.

Peer influence is another significant factor in the development of sexual attraction in children. As children grow older, they seek validation and acceptance from their peers, which can impact their attitudes towards sexuality. Peer pressure and the desire to fit in can lead children to engage in risky sexual behaviors or develop unhealthy attitudes towards sexuality. Educators, along with parents, should focus on promoting positive peer relationships and fostering a supportive environment where children can make informed decisions about their own sexual attraction.

In conclusion, cultural variations in attitudes towards sexuality greatly influence the development of sexual attraction in children. Parents and educators must recognize and understand these cultural influences to provide appropriate guidance and support to children. By addressing the role of media, fostering open communication, and promoting positive peer relationships, parents and educators can help children develop healthy attitudes towards sexuality and navigate this crucial aspect of their development.

Religious Beliefs and Their Impact on Children's Understanding of Attraction

Religious beliefs play a significant role in shaping a child's understanding of attraction and can greatly influence their development in this area. As parents and educators, it is crucial to understand how religious teachings impact children's perception of attraction and guide them towards healthy attitudes and behaviors.

One key factor is the emphasis on abstinence until marriage in many religious communities. This belief promotes a conservative approach to sexuality and can lead children to view attraction as something to be suppressed or avoided altogether. While abstinence is a valid choice, it is essential to balance this teaching with a comprehensive understanding of healthy relationships and consent.

Moreover, religious teachings often convey a specific set of moral values regarding attraction and relationships. Children may be taught that attraction is natural but should only be expressed within the confines of a heterosexual, monogamous marriage. This can create confusion and shame for children who experience or develop attractions that do not align with these teachings, such as same-sex attractions or non-binary identities.

It is essential for parents and educators to create a safe and inclusive environment where children can openly discuss their feelings and questions about attraction, irrespective of their religious backgrounds. By fostering open dialogue, children can gain a better understanding of their own attractions and beliefs while respecting the diversity of others.

Additionally, religious communities can play a pivotal role in supporting children's understanding of attraction. Religious leaders and educators should be trained to provide accurate and age-appropriate information about attraction, relationships, and consent. They can also emphasize the importance of empathy, respect, and acceptance towards individuals with different attractions or identities.

While religious beliefs can shape a child's understanding of attraction, it is crucial to strike a balance between religious teachings and a comprehensive, inclusive education. Parents and educators must ensure that children are equipped with accurate information, empathy, and respect for diversity. By addressing the impact of religious beliefs on children's understanding of attraction, we can foster a healthier environment for their sexual development and promote a more inclusive society overall.

Navigating Cross-Cultural Influences in a Globalized World

In today's globalized world, children are exposed to a myriad of cross-cultural influences that shape their development, including their sexual attraction. As parents and educators, it is crucial to understand these factors and their impact on children's sexual attraction to provide guidance and support. This subchapter delves into the complex interplay of various cultural influences and provides insights on how to navigate them effectively.

One of the key factors influencing the development of sexual attraction in children is the role of media and technology. With the widespread availability of media, children are exposed to a range of sexualized content at a young age. This exposure can shape their understanding of relationships, gender roles, and even their own body image. Parents and educators must be proactive in monitoring and limiting children's exposure to age-inappropriate media, while also engaging in open and honest conversations about healthy relationships and boundaries.

Cultural influences also play a significant role in shaping children's sexual attraction. Different cultures have varying norms and values surrounding sexuality, which can impact how children perceive and express their attraction. Understanding cultural nuances and having open discussions about these differences is vital to ensure children develop a healthy and respectful understanding of sexual attraction.

Parental guidance is another crucial aspect of supporting children's healthy sexual attraction development. Parents need to create a safe and open environment where children can ask questions and seek guidance without fear of judgment. By providing accurate information and age-appropriate education on sexuality, parents can help children build a strong foundation for their understanding of sexual attraction.

Peer influence is also a powerful force in shaping children's sexual attraction. Friends and social circles can contribute to the development of certain attitudes and behaviors regarding sexuality. Encouraging positive peer relationships and fostering conversations about healthy relationships and consent can help mitigate any negative influences.

Psychological and emotional factors can also influence sexual attraction development. Factors such as self-esteem, body image, and past experiences can impact how children perceive themselves and others. Promoting positive self-image and addressing any emotional concerns can support healthy sexual attraction development.

Education and awareness programs are crucial in promoting healthy sexual attraction development in children. Schools and communities should provide comprehensive sex education programs that address consent, healthy relationships, and respect for diversity. By equipping children with knowledge and skills, we can empower them to navigate their own sexual attractions in a safe and healthy manner.

Early childhood experiences, neurological, and hormonal factors also contribute to the development of sexual attraction. Understanding these factors can help parents and educators identify any potential concerns and intervene early on when necessary.

Finally, this subchapter explores intervention strategies for addressing inappropriate sexual attraction in children. It emphasizes the importance of seeking professional help and guidance when faced with challenging situations, as well as the need for a supportive and non-judgmental approach.

In conclusion, navigating cross-cultural influences in a globalized world is essential for parents and educators in understanding and supporting the development of sexual attraction in children. By being aware of the factors influencing sexual attraction, fostering open communication, and providing accurate information, we can help children navigate their own sexual attractions in a healthy and respectful manner.

Chapter 6: Parental Guidance and Its Impact on the Development of Sexual Attraction in Children

Open Communication and Creating a Safe Space for Discussion

In the complex landscape of understanding the factors shaping sexual attraction in children, open communication and creating a safe space for discussion play a crucial role. As parents and educators, it is our responsibility to foster an environment where children feel comfortable expressing their thoughts, concerns, and questions about their developing sexual attraction.

Research shows that open communication is essential for healthy sexual development in children. By encouraging dialogue, we provide them with the tools to navigate their feelings and understand their experiences. This subchapter will explore the significance of open communication and the creation of a safe space for discussion in addressing the factors shaping sexual attraction in children.

One of the key factors influencing the development of sexual attraction in children is the role of media and technology. By maintaining an open line of communication, parents and educators can help children critically analyze media messages, challenge unrealistic expectations, and understand the difference between healthy relationships and harmful stereotypes.

Cultural influences also play a significant role in shaping sexual attraction in children. By encouraging open conversations about diverse cultural beliefs and values, we can help children develop a broader understanding of sexuality and respect for different perspectives.

Moreover, parental guidance is crucial in shaping children's sexual attraction development. By creating a safe space for discussion, parents can provide accurate information, address misconceptions, and instill values that promote healthy relationships and consent.

Peer influence is another factor that cannot be overlooked. By fostering open communication, we can help children navigate peer pressure, establish boundaries, and make informed decisions about their sexual attraction.

Psychological and emotional factors also influence the development of sexual attraction in children. By encouraging open discussions, parents and educators can provide support, address any concerns, and help children build a healthy self-image and self-esteem.

Education and awareness programs play a vital role in promoting healthy sexual attraction development in children. By engaging in open dialogue, parents and educators can reinforce the knowledge gained from these programs, answer questions, and address any misconceptions.

Early childhood experiences have a profound impact on the development of sexual attraction. By creating a safe space for discussion, parents and educators can help children process any negative experiences, promote healing, and ensure healthy development.

Furthermore, understanding the neurological and hormonal factors affecting sexual attraction is crucial. By discussing these topics openly, parents and educators can provide a scientific understanding of these factors while addressing any concerns or questions children may have.

Lastly, this subchapter will explore intervention strategies for addressing inappropriate sexual attraction in children. By maintaining an open line of communication, parents and educators can identify warning signs, seek professional help when necessary, and provide the support and guidance needed to address these issues effectively.

In conclusion, open communication and creating a safe space for discussion are foundational in understanding the factors shaping sexual attraction in children. By fostering an environment where children feel heard, supported, and informed, parents and educators can play a critical role in their healthy sexual development.

Age-Appropriate Sex Education and Conversations

In today's modern world, the development of sexual attraction in children is a topic that cannot be ignored. As parents and educators, it is our responsibility to understand the factors that shape sexual attraction in children and to provide them with the guidance they need to navigate this complex aspect of their lives. This subchapter will delve into the importance of age-appropriate sex education and conversations and how they play a crucial role in the healthy development of sexual attraction in children.

One of the key factors influencing the development of sexual attraction in children is the role of media and technology. From television shows to social media platforms, children are exposed to a wide range of explicit content that can shape their understanding of sexuality. It is vital for parents and educators to be aware of the media that children consume and to engage in open conversations about the messages they are receiving.

Cultural influences also play a significant role in the development of sexual attraction in children. Different cultures have varying attitudes and beliefs about sexuality, and these can impact how children perceive and understand their own feelings. By acknowledging and respecting cultural differences, parents and educators can provide a more comprehensive and inclusive sex education to children.

Parental guidance is another crucial factor in the development of sexual attraction in children. Parents have a unique opportunity to shape their child's understanding of sexuality by engaging in open and honest conversations. By creating a safe and judgment-free environment, parents can foster healthy attitudes towards sexuality and provide accurate information that dispels myths and misconceptions.

Peer influence is another aspect that cannot be overlooked. As children grow older, their friends and peers become increasingly influential in shaping their attitudes and behaviors. It is important for parents and educators to encourage positive peer relationships and to provide guidance on healthy boundaries and consent.

Psychological and emotional factors also play a significant role in the development of sexual attraction in children. Children who have experienced trauma or have low self-esteem may be more vulnerable to inappropriate sexual attraction. By addressing these underlying issues through therapy and counseling, parents and educators can help children develop healthier attitudes towards sexuality.

Education and awareness programs are essential for promoting healthy sexual attraction development in children. Schools and community organizations play a vital role in providing comprehensive sex education that is age-appropriate and inclusive. By equipping children with accurate information and teaching them about consent and healthy relationships, we can empower them to make informed choices.

Early childhood experiences can also have a lasting impact on the development of sexual attraction. Trauma or negative experiences during this critical period can shape a child's understanding of sexuality. It is crucial for parents and educators to provide support and therapy when needed to address any issues that may arise.

Finally, neurological and hormonal factors cannot be ignored. Children go through significant changes in their brain and body during puberty, which can influence their sexual attraction. By understanding these factors, parents and educators can provide the necessary support and information to help children navigate these changes.

In conclusion, age-appropriate sex education and conversations are essential in the healthy development of sexual attraction in children. By being aware of the various factors that shape sexual attraction, parents and educators can provide the guidance and support that children need to navigate this aspect of their lives. Through open and honest conversations, education programs, and addressing underlying psychological and emotional issues, we can empower children to develop healthy attitudes towards sexuality and make informed choices.

Addressing Parental Anxiety and Taboos Around Sexual Attraction

As parents and educators, it is crucial to understand the factors that shape sexual attraction in children. This subchapter aims to address the parental anxiety and taboos surrounding this topic, providing valuable insights and guidance to navigate this sensitive area.

The development of sexual attraction in children is a complex process influenced by various factors. Understanding these factors is essential for creating a safe and supportive environment for our children. Factors such as biological, psychological, and social aspects play a role in shaping their sexual attractions.

One prominent factor is the role of media and technology. In today's digital age, children are exposed to a vast amount of explicit content, which can influence their understanding of sexuality. Parents must be vigilant in monitoring and regulating their children's media consumption to ensure they receive accurate and age-appropriate information.

Cultural influences also impact the development of sexual attraction. Different societies have varying norms and values surrounding sexuality. Parents and educators must engage in open and honest discussions about these cultural influences, promoting tolerance and respect for diversity.

Parental guidance plays a crucial role in shaping a child's understanding of sexual attraction. Parents should establish open lines of communication, providing accurate information and addressing any concerns or questions their children may have. By fostering a safe and non-judgmental environment, parents can help alleviate anxiety and create a healthy understanding of sexuality.

Peer influence is another significant factor in the development of sexual attraction. Children often look to their peers for guidance and validation. Educators and parents should promote positive peer relationships and encourage open dialogue, enabling children to navigate their feelings and experiences in a supportive environment.

Psychological and emotional factors also influence sexual attraction in children. Past traumas or experiences can impact their understanding of relationships and attraction. It is essential to address and support children who may have experienced any form of abuse or trauma, seeking professional help when necessary.

Education and awareness programs are vital for healthy sexual attraction development. Schools and parents should collaborate to implement comprehensive sex education programs that provide accurate information, promote consent, and teach children about healthy relationships.

Early childhood experiences can have a lasting impact on the development of sexual attraction. Parents should create a nurturing and secure environment, promoting healthy boundaries and teaching children about consent from an early age.

Neurological and hormonal factors also affect sexual attraction development. Understanding the biological aspects can help parents and educators explain the physical changes children experience during puberty, reducing anxiety and promoting understanding.

Finally, intervention strategies for addressing inappropriate sexual attraction in children should be discussed. If a child exhibits concerning behaviors, seeking professional help is crucial to ensure their well-being and provide appropriate guidance.

By addressing parental anxiety and taboos surrounding sexual attraction, parents and educators can create an open and supportive environment for children to develop a healthy understanding of their sexuality.

Chapter 7: Peer Influence and the Development of Sexual Attraction in Children

Understanding the Power of Peer Influence

Peer influence plays a significant role in shaping the development of sexual attraction in children. As parents and educators, it is crucial to recognize and understand the power of peer influence and its impact on our children's perceptions and behaviors.

During the developmental stage, children start forming friendships and engaging in social interactions with their peers. These peer interactions provide opportunities for children to learn from each other, share experiences, and form their own opinions. However, when it comes to sexual attraction, peer influence can have both positive and negative effects.

Positive peer influence can involve healthy discussions, mutual respect, and open communication about sexual attraction. It can help children gain a better understanding of themselves, their bodies, and their feelings. Positive peer influence can also promote healthy relationships, consent, and respect for boundaries.

On the other hand, negative peer influence can lead to risky behaviors and unhealthy attitudes towards sexual attraction. Peer pressure can push children into engaging in sexual activities before they are ready or comfortable. It can also promote unhealthy stereotypes, objectification, and unrealistic expectations regarding sexual attraction.

Media and technology play a significant role in peer influence, as children are increasingly exposed to a wide range of content through television, movies, social media, and the internet. These platforms often depict unrealistic and hypersexualized images and messages, which can distort children's perceptions of sexual attraction.

Cultural influences also play a crucial role in shaping children's understanding of sexual attraction. Different cultures have varying norms, values, and beliefs regarding sexual attraction and relationships. It is essential for parents and educators to engage in open dialogues about cultural diversity, respect, and acceptance to help children develop a healthy understanding of sexual attraction in different contexts.

Parental guidance is an essential factor in mitigating the negative impacts of peer influence. By providing age-appropriate information, fostering open communication, and setting clear boundaries, parents can help their children navigate peer pressure and make informed decisions about sexual attraction.

Educators also play a vital role in promoting healthy sexual attraction development. Schools can implement comprehensive sex education programs that address consent, healthy relationships, and the influence of media and culture. Such programs can empower children to make responsible choices and develop a positive attitude towards sexual attraction.

In conclusion, understanding the power of peer influence is crucial in navigating the development of sexual attraction in children. Parents and educators must be aware of the positive and negative aspects of peer influence and work towards creating a supportive environment that promotes healthy discussions, respect for boundaries, and informed decision-making. By doing so, we can help our children develop a healthy understanding of sexual attraction and equip them with the necessary tools to navigate their relationships in a responsible and respectful manner.

Exploring the Impact of Friendships and Peer Pressure on Sexual Attraction

Friendships and peer pressure play a significant role in shaping the development of sexual attraction in children. As parents and educators, it is crucial for us to understand and acknowledge these influences to provide appropriate guidance and support to our children. In this subchapter, we will delve into the impact of friendships and peer pressure on the development of sexual attraction in children.

During childhood and adolescence, friendships and peer relationships become increasingly important in a child's life. These relationships often serve as a platform for exploring and understanding their own identity, including their sexual attraction. Friends can influence each other's thoughts, feelings, and behaviors, including their perspectives on sexuality.

Peer pressure is a significant factor that can shape a child's sexual attraction. Children may feel compelled to conform to their peers' expectations and ideals regarding attractiveness and desirability. This pressure can contribute to the formation of unhealthy or inappropriate sexual attractions. It is essential for parents and educators to educate children about the importance of respecting boundaries, consent, and healthy relationships to counteract negative peer influences.

Media and technology also heavily influence the development of sexual attraction in children. Friends often share and discuss media content, including movies, TV shows, music, and online content, which can shape their perceptions of attractiveness and relationships. Parents and educators must monitor and guide children's media consumption to ensure they are exposed to age-appropriate and healthy representations of sexuality.

Cultural influences also play a role in shaping a child's sexual attraction. Different cultures have different norms and expectations regarding sexuality, which can influence a child's understanding and acceptance of their own attractions. It is crucial for parents and educators to foster an open and inclusive environment that celebrates diversity and promotes understanding of different cultural perspectives.

Parental guidance is vital in helping children navigate their sexual attractions. Open and honest communication between parents and children can provide a safe space for children to ask questions, express concerns, and seek guidance. Parents should strive to create an environment where children feel comfortable discussing their feelings and experiences without fear of judgment or punishment.

In conclusion, friendships and peer pressure have a significant impact on the development of sexual attraction in children. Parents and educators must be aware of these influences and provide appropriate guidance and support to help children navigate their sexual attractions in a healthy and informed manner. By fostering open communication, monitoring media consumption, and promoting cultural understanding, we can create an environment that supports the development of healthy and respectful sexual attraction in children.

Strategies for Promoting Positive Peer Relationships and Healthy Boundaries

In the journey of a child's development, the establishment of positive peer relationships and healthy boundaries is crucial. As parents and educators, it is our role to equip children with the necessary strategies to navigate these relationships in a safe and respectful manner. By fostering positive peer relationships, we can help children develop a strong foundation for healthy social interactions and emotional well-being. Here are some effective strategies to promote positive peer relationships and healthy boundaries in children:

1. Encourage open communication: Create an environment where children feel comfortable expressing their thoughts and emotions. Encourage them to communicate openly with their peers, discussing their feelings and resolving conflicts through respectful dialogue.

2. Teach empathy and respect: Help children understand the importance of empathy and respect towards others. Encourage them to consider different perspectives and appreciate diversity, fostering a culture of inclusiveness and tolerance.

3. Set clear boundaries: Establish clear boundaries and guidelines for appropriate behavior. Teach children to recognize and respect personal boundaries, promoting mutual respect and consent.

4. Foster cooperation and teamwork: Engage children in activities that promote cooperation and teamwork. Encourage them to work together towards common goals, promoting a sense of belonging and shared responsibility.

5. Provide guidance on media literacy: In today's digital age, media and technology play a significant role in shaping children's perception of sexual attraction. Educate children about media literacy, teaching them to critically analyze and question the messages they encounter, promoting healthy attitudes towards relationships and sexuality.

6. Promote self-esteem and self-confidence: Help children build a positive self-image and develop self-confidence. Encourage them to embrace their unique qualities and strengths, fostering resilience and assertiveness when facing peer pressure.

7. Teach problem-solving skills: Equip children with problem-solving skills to navigate conflicts and challenges in peer relationships. Teach them effective communication, negotiation, and compromise techniques, empowering them to resolve conflicts constructively.

8. Encourage healthy friendships: Encourage children to seek out friendships based on shared interests, mutual respect, and positive values. Help them understand the qualities of healthy friendships and discourage toxic or manipulative relationships.

9. Provide age-appropriate sex education: As children grow older, it is essential to provide age-appropriate sex education. This education should include information about consent, healthy relationships, boundaries, and understanding sexual attraction in a context that is appropriate for their developmental stage.

10. Be a positive role model: Model positive peer relationships and healthy boundaries in your own interactions. Children learn from observing adults, so demonstrate respectful communication, empathy, and healthy conflict resolution strategies.

By implementing these strategies, parents and educators can play a crucial role in promoting positive peer relationships and healthy boundaries. Creating a supportive environment that fosters open communication, empathy, and respect will empower children to develop healthy attitudes towards relationships and navigate the complexities of sexual attraction in a safe and responsible manner.

Chapter 8: Psychological and Emotional Factors Influencing Sexual Attraction in Children

Self-Identity and Sexual Orientation

Understanding the Factors Shaping Sexual Attraction in Children: A Parent's Perspective

In today's rapidly evolving society, it is essential for parents and educators to have a comprehensive understanding of the factors that shape sexual attraction in children. One crucial aspect of this understanding is recognizing the significance of self-identity and sexual orientation in a child's development. This subchapter delves into the intricacies of self-identity and sexual orientation, shedding light on how these factors influence the development of sexual attraction in children.

Self-identity is an integral part of a child's overall development, including their sexual orientation. As children grow and explore their own individuality, they begin to form a sense of self-identity, which encompasses their gender identity and sexual orientation. It is important to note that self-identity and sexual orientation may manifest differently in each child, and they may not align with societal norms or expectations. As parents and educators, it is crucial to create an inclusive and accepting environment where children feel safe to explore and express their self-identity.

Factors influencing the development of sexual attraction in children go beyond self-identity. The role of media and technology cannot be overlooked in shaping children's understanding of sexuality. The constant exposure to sexualized content and unrealistic portrayals of relationships can have a profound impact on a child's perception of sexual attraction. As parents and educators, it is essential to monitor and guide children's media consumption, providing them with accurate and age-appropriate information.

Cultural influences also play a significant role in the development of sexual attraction in children. Different cultures have varying attitudes towards sexuality, which can shape a child's understanding and acceptance of their own sexual orientation. Parents and educators must be aware of these cultural influences and strive to create an inclusive environment that respects and celebrates diversity in all its forms.

Parental guidance is paramount in supporting the healthy development of sexual attraction in children. By engaging in open and honest conversations about sexuality, parents can provide their children with the knowledge and understanding they need to navigate their feelings and emotions. Additionally, peer influence can impact a child's understanding of sexual attraction. Encouraging healthy friendships and fostering open dialogue about sexuality can help children develop a balanced perspective.

Psychological and emotional factors also play a role in influencing sexual attraction in children. Understanding a child's emotional well-being and providing appropriate support can positively impact their overall sexual development. Education and awareness programs can further enhance a child's understanding of healthy sexual attraction, promoting positive self-identity and self-acceptance.

Early childhood experiences, including exposure to trauma or abuse, can have a lasting impact on a child's development of sexual attraction. It is crucial for parents and educators to be sensitive to these experiences and provide appropriate intervention strategies to address any inappropriate sexual attraction in children. Recognizing the neurological and hormonal factors that affect sexual attraction can also aid in understanding a child's development and addressing any concerns.

In conclusion, self-identity and sexual orientation are critical factors in shaping sexual attraction in children. By fostering an inclusive and accepting environment, providing accurate information, and addressing the various influences on a child's development, parents and educators can support healthy sexual attraction development in children. This subchapter aims to equip parents and educators with the knowledge and tools necessary to navigate this complex aspect of a child's development.

Body Image and Self-Esteem

In today's society, body image and self-esteem play a significant role in the development of sexual attraction in children. As parents and educators, it is crucial to understand the factors that shape these aspects of a child's life and how they can impact their overall well-being.

One significant factor that influences body image and self-esteem is the role of media and technology. Children are constantly bombarded with unrealistic beauty standards and idealized body types through social media, television, and advertisements. This can lead to feelings of inadequacy and low self-esteem, as children compare themselves to these unattainable standards. As parents and educators, we must teach children to critically analyze media messages and promote positive body image by celebrating diversity and individuality.

Cultural influences also play a significant role in shaping body image and self-esteem. Different cultures have different beauty ideals, and children may face pressure to conform to these standards. It is essential to educate children about cultural diversity and teach them to embrace and celebrate their own unique traits.

Parental guidance is crucial in shaping a child's body image and self-esteem. Parents should provide positive reinforcement, encourage open communication, and promote a healthy body image by emphasizing the importance of inner qualities and self-acceptance. By fostering a supportive and accepting environment, parents can help children develop a positive self-image and strong self-esteem.

Peer influence is another factor that can impact body image and self-esteem. Children may feel pressure to conform to their peers' expectations, which can lead to unhealthy behaviors and negative body image. It is essential for parents and educators to foster healthy relationships and teach children to value themselves for who they are, rather than seeking validation from others.

Psychological and emotional factors also play a significant role in shaping body image and self-esteem. Children who have experienced trauma or have low self-esteem may be more susceptible to developing negative body image issues. It is crucial to address these underlying psychological and emotional factors through therapy or counseling to promote healthy development.

Education and awareness programs can play a vital role in promoting healthy sexual attraction development in children. By providing accurate and age-appropriate information about body image, self-esteem, and healthy relationships, parents and educators can empower children to make informed choices and develop a positive sense of self.

Early childhood experiences, including positive or negative interactions with caregivers, can also influence a child's body image and self-esteem. It is crucial to provide a nurturing and supportive environment during these formative years to promote healthy development.

Neurological and hormonal factors also affect the development of sexual attraction in children. It is crucial to understand these biological processes and their impact on a child's development to provide appropriate support and guidance.

In cases where inappropriate sexual attraction emerges in children, intervention strategies must be implemented. This may include seeking professional help from therapists or counselors who specialize in addressing these issues. It is essential to approach the situation with sensitivity and provide a safe space for the child to express their feelings and concerns.

In conclusion, body image and self-esteem significantly influence the development of sexual attraction in children. By understanding the various factors at play, parents and educators can create a nurturing and supportive environment that promotes healthy development and positive self-image in children.

Trauma and its Effects on Sexual Attraction Development

Trauma can have a profound impact on the development of sexual attraction in children. Whether it is experiencing physical, emotional, or sexual abuse, witnessing violence, or going through a significant life event, trauma can leave lasting scars on a child's psyche, including their understanding and experience of sexual attraction.

Children who have experienced trauma may exhibit various behaviors that can be linked to their sexual attraction development. It is important for parents and educators to understand these effects and provide appropriate support and guidance to help children navigate their feelings and experiences in a healthy and safe manner.

One common effect of trauma on sexual attraction development is the distortion of boundaries. Children who have experienced trauma might struggle with understanding appropriate boundaries in relationships, leading to confusion and potential vulnerability to exploitation. It is crucial for parents and educators to teach children about consent, personal boundaries, and healthy relationships to counteract these effects.

Trauma can also impact a child's self-esteem and body image, which can influence how they perceive and relate to others sexually. Children who have experienced trauma may develop negative beliefs about themselves, leading to difficulties in forming healthy and positive connections with others. It is essential for parents and educators to promote a positive self-image and provide opportunities for children to develop healthy self-esteem.

Moreover, trauma can affect a child's ability to trust and form secure attachments. This can manifest in the way a child views relationships and influences their sexual attraction development. Parents and educators should create a safe and supportive environment where children can build trust and form healthy attachments with peers and adults.

It is worth noting that trauma can have varying effects on different children. Some may exhibit heightened sexual attraction, while others may display a decreased interest or aversion to sexual experiences. Therefore, it is essential to approach each child's experience individually and provide tailored support to meet their unique needs.

In conclusion, trauma can significantly impact the development of sexual attraction in children. It is crucial for parents and educators to be aware of the effects of trauma and provide appropriate guidance and support. By understanding the factors shaping sexual attraction development, such as trauma, we can work towards creating a safe and healthy environment for children to explore and understand their feelings and experiences.

Chapter 9: Education and Awareness Programs for Healthy Sexual Attraction Development in Children

School-Based Sex Education Programs

Sex education plays a crucial role in the healthy development of children's sexual attraction. As parents and educators, it is our responsibility to provide them with accurate information and guidance to navigate this aspect of their lives. School-based sex education programs have proven to be an effective way to address the various factors that influence the development of sexual attraction in children.

One of the key factors influencing children's sexual attraction is the role of media and technology. With easy access to explicit content, it is essential to teach children how to critically analyze and interpret what they see. School-based programs can educate children about media literacy and help them understand the difference between healthy relationships and harmful stereotypes portrayed in the media.

Cultural influences also play a significant role in shaping sexual attraction. By including discussions on diverse cultural perspectives, school-based programs can promote tolerance and understanding. This helps children develop a broader understanding of sexuality and reduces the likelihood of negative stereotypes or biases.

Parental guidance is crucial in the development of sexual attraction in children. School-based programs can work in conjunction with parents to provide information and resources to support open and honest conversations at home. By involving parents in these programs, we ensure that the information provided at school aligns with the values and beliefs of families.

Peer influence is another critical factor in children's sexual attraction. School-based programs can foster a supportive environment where children can discuss and learn from their peers. By promoting healthy relationships and consent, these programs empower children to make informed decisions and resist peer pressure.

Psychological and emotional factors also play a significant role in the development of sexual attraction. School-based programs can provide a safe space for children to discuss their feelings and emotions. By addressing topics such as body image, self-esteem, and mental health, these programs help children develop a positive sense of self and healthier relationships.

Education and awareness programs for healthy sexual attraction development in children are essential. By providing age-appropriate information on topics such as consent, boundaries, and reproductive health, school-based programs equip children with the knowledge and skills they need to make responsible decisions.

Early childhood experiences can have a lasting impact on the development of sexual attraction. School-based programs can provide support and resources for children who may have experienced trauma or abuse. By addressing these issues in a sensitive and age-appropriate manner, we can help children heal and develop healthy relationships.

Neurological and hormonal factors also affect the development of sexual attraction in children. School-based programs can provide accurate scientific information on these topics, dispelling myths and misconceptions. This helps children understand the biological aspects of their sexual development and promotes a healthy body image.

In cases where inappropriate sexual attraction is observed, intervention strategies are crucial. School-based programs can train educators to identify signs of inappropriate behavior and provide resources for intervention and support. By addressing these issues early on, we can help children navigate their feelings and prevent harmful actions.

In conclusion, school-based sex education programs are a valuable tool for parents and educators in promoting healthy sexual attraction development in children. By addressing the various factors influencing sexual attraction, these programs equip children with the knowledge, skills, and support they need to make informed decisions and develop healthy relationships.

Community Initiatives and Resources for Parents and Educators

In today's rapidly evolving world, parents and educators play a crucial role in understanding and addressing the factors shaping sexual attraction in children. While this topic may be uncomfortable or daunting, it is essential to equip ourselves with the knowledge and resources needed to guide children through this aspect of their development. Fortunately, there are numerous community initiatives and resources available that can support parents and educators in this endeavor.

One of the key factors influencing the development of sexual attraction in children is the role of media and technology. To address this, community organizations often organize workshops and seminars aimed at educating parents and educators about the impact of media on children's sexual development. These initiatives provide practical strategies for limiting exposure to inappropriate content and promoting healthy media consumption habits.

Cultural influences also play a significant role in shaping children's sexual attraction. Community organizations often collaborate with cultural and religious institutions to develop culturally sensitive resources and programs. These initiatives aim to foster open dialogue within families and communities, encouraging parents and educators to address sexual attraction in a manner that aligns with their cultural values.

Parental guidance is crucial in shaping healthy sexual attraction development in children. Community centers frequently offer support groups and counseling services for parents, creating a safe space for discussions and sharing experiences. These initiatives provide parents and educators with the opportunity to learn from experts and connect with other individuals facing similar challenges.

Peer influence is another factor that cannot be ignored. Community organizations often collaborate with schools to implement peer education programs. These initiatives empower young people to become advocates for healthy sexual attraction development, equipping them with the knowledge and skills to engage in respectful and responsible relationships.

Psychological and emotional factors also play a significant role in children's sexual attraction development. Community initiatives often provide access to mental health professionals who can offer guidance and support to parents and educators. By addressing underlying psychological and emotional issues, these initiatives contribute to fostering healthy sexual attraction development in children.

Education and awareness programs are crucial for promoting healthy sexual attraction development in children. Community organizations often partner with schools and healthcare providers to deliver age-appropriate and evidence-based sexual education curricula. These programs aim to provide children with accurate information, challenge harmful stereotypes, and promote healthy relationships.

Early childhood experiences have a lasting impact on the development of sexual attraction. Community initiatives often focus on providing support to families and caregivers, offering resources and guidance on creating safe and nurturing environments for children. These initiatives emphasize the importance of healthy attachment and positive relationships in shaping children's sexual development.

Neurological and hormonal factors also influence the development of sexual attraction in children. Community organizations often collaborate with healthcare professionals to provide workshops and seminars on the biological aspects of sexual development. These initiatives aim to empower parents and educators with a scientific understanding of the topic, enabling them to address children's questions and concerns effectively.

In cases where inappropriate sexual attraction arises, community initiatives offer intervention strategies. These resources often include guidelines for recognizing signs of inappropriate behavior and seeking appropriate professional help. By providing parents and educators with the tools to address such situations, these initiatives protect children from potential harm and promote their healthy development.

In conclusion, community initiatives and resources play a vital role in supporting parents and educators in understanding and addressing the factors shaping sexual attraction in children. By actively engaging in these initiatives, parents and educators can equip themselves with the knowledge and resources needed to navigate this complex aspect of children's development successfully. Together, we can create a supportive and nurturing environment that promotes healthy sexual attraction development in children.

Promoting Consent and Respectful Relationships in Educational Settings

In today's society, it is crucial for parents and educators to understand the factors shaping sexual attraction in children and their role in promoting healthy development. This subchapter aims to shed light on the importance of consent and respectful relationships in educational settings.

One of the key factors influencing the development of sexual attraction in children is their exposure to media and technology. With the rise of digital platforms, children are consuming a vast amount of content that can shape their perceptions of relationships and consent. Therefore, it becomes essential for parents and educators to monitor and guide their children's media consumption, ensuring they are exposed to age-appropriate content that promotes healthy relationships.

Cultural influences also play a significant role in shaping sexual attraction in children. Different cultures have varying norms and values surrounding relationships, gender roles, and consent. It is essential for parents and educators to be aware of these cultural influences and provide children with a comprehensive understanding of consent and respectful relationships that transcends cultural boundaries.

Parental guidance is another crucial factor in the development of sexual attraction in children. Open and honest communication between parents and children about relationships, boundaries, and consent is vital. Parents should encourage their children to ask questions, express their feelings, and set boundaries. By providing guidance and support, parents can help children develop a healthy understanding of consent and respectful relationships.

Peer influence also plays a significant role in shaping sexual attraction in children. Educators need to create a safe and inclusive environment where children can openly discuss and learn about relationships and consent. Peer education programs can be implemented to encourage dialogue and facilitate understanding among children.

Psychological and emotional factors must also be considered when addressing sexual attraction in children. Traumatic experiences, such as abuse or neglect, can impact a child's perception of relationships and consent. Intervention strategies should focus on providing therapeutic support and counseling to help children heal and develop healthy attitudes towards relationships.

Education and awareness programs are essential tools for promoting healthy sexual attraction development in children. These programs should be implemented in educational settings to teach children about consent, boundaries, and healthy relationships. By providing children with accurate and age-appropriate information, educators can empower them to make informed choices and foster respectful relationships.

Early childhood experiences also have a significant impact on the development of sexual attraction. Children who experience secure and nurturing relationships are more likely to develop healthy attitudes towards relationships and consent. Therefore, parents and educators must create a supportive environment that nurtures emotional well-being and encourages positive relationship-building skills.

Understanding the neurological and hormonal factors affecting the development of sexual attraction in children is crucial. Educators should stay informed about the latest research in this field to ensure they can provide accurate information and support to children.

In conclusion, promoting consent and respectful relationships in educational settings is vital for the healthy development of children's sexual attraction. By understanding the various factors that influence sexual attraction and implementing appropriate intervention strategies, parents and educators can create a safe and inclusive environment that fosters healthy attitudes towards relationships, boundaries, and consent.

Chapter 10: Impact of Early Childhood Experiences on the Development of Sexual Attraction

Attachment Theory and Its Influence on Attraction Development

Attachment theory is a psychological framework that explores the formation of emotional bonds between children and their caregivers. This theory suggests that early experiences in relationships can have a significant impact on the development of an individual's social and emotional functioning throughout their lives. In the context of sexual attraction, attachment theory provides valuable insights into how children form relationships and develop their understanding of attraction.

The development of sexual attraction in children is a complex process influenced by various factors. One of the key factors is the quality of attachment formed in early childhood. Secure attachments, characterized by consistent and responsive caregiving, promote a sense of trust and emotional security in children. These children are more likely to develop healthy relationships and a positive understanding of attraction later in life.

On the other hand, insecure attachments, such as those characterized by neglect or inconsistent caregiving, can have adverse effects on the development of sexual attraction. Children who experience insecure attachments may struggle with forming healthy relationships, have difficulty understanding boundaries, or display inappropriate sexual behaviors. It is crucial for parents and educators to recognize the importance of secure attachment in promoting healthy attraction development.

The role of media and technology cannot be ignored in today's digital age. Children are exposed to a wide range of media content, including sexualized images and messages. This exposure can shape their understanding of attraction and influence their behaviors. Parents and educators must be vigilant in monitoring and guiding children's media consumption, promoting age-appropriate content, and engaging in open conversations about healthy relationships and consent.

Cultural influences also play a significant role in the development of sexual attraction in children. Each culture has its own norms, values, and beliefs regarding relationships and attraction. Parents and educators need to be aware of these cultural influences and provide guidance that aligns with their values while promoting respect for diversity and consent.

Parental guidance is crucial in shaping children's understanding of attraction. Open and honest communication about relationships, boundaries, and consent is essential. Parents should create a safe space for children to ask questions and express their feelings without judgment. Education and awareness programs can also support parents in navigating these conversations effectively.

Peer influence is another important factor in attraction development. As children grow older, their peers become increasingly influential in shaping their understanding of relationships and attraction. Parents and educators should encourage positive peer relationships and provide guidance on healthy boundaries and respectful behavior.

Psychological and emotional factors can significantly influence sexual attraction development. Children with a strong sense of self-esteem and self-worth are more likely to form healthy relationships and make informed choices regarding attraction. It is important to foster a positive self-image and promote emotional well-being in children.

Early childhood experiences can have a lasting impact on the development of sexual attraction. Traumatic or abusive experiences can disrupt healthy attachment and influence children's understanding of relationships and attraction. Early intervention and appropriate support are crucial in addressing the effects of such experiences and promoting healthy development.

Neurological and hormonal factors also play a role in attraction development. As children enter puberty, hormonal changes can influence their feelings and behaviors. Parents and educators should provide age-appropriate education about these changes, emphasizing the importance of consent and respectful behavior.

Finally, intervention strategies are necessary when addressing inappropriate sexual attraction in children. Early identification and appropriate support can help children understand boundaries, develop healthy relationships, and prevent harmful behaviors. Professional guidance from therapists or counselors may be beneficial in addressing complex issues.

In conclusion, understanding the factors shaping sexual attraction in children requires a comprehensive approach that considers attachment theory, media influence, cultural influences, parental guidance, peer influence, psychological and emotional factors, education and awareness programs, early childhood experiences, neurological and hormonal factors, and intervention strategies. By addressing these factors, parents and educators can play a crucial role in promoting healthy sexual attraction development in children and ensuring their overall well-being.

Parent-Child Bonding and its Long-Term Effects on Sexual Attraction

The parent-child bond is a crucial aspect of a child's development, influencing various aspects of their lives, including their sexual attraction. Understanding the factors shaping sexual attraction in children is essential for parents and educators to provide appropriate guidance and support.

Research suggests that a strong parent-child bond has a significant impact on the development of sexual attraction in children. When children feel loved, accepted, and valued by their parents, they develop a secure attachment, which positively influences their self-esteem and body image. This, in turn, plays a role in shaping their sexual attraction as they grow older.

Positive parent-child relationships also foster open communication. When children feel comfortable discussing their feelings and experiences with their parents, they are more likely to seek guidance and support when it comes to navigating their emerging sexual attraction. This open dialogue allows parents to provide accurate information, address concerns, and promote healthy attitudes towards sexuality.

Furthermore, parental guidance is crucial in helping children develop appropriate boundaries and understanding consent. Parents can teach their children about personal space, respect for others, and the importance of obtaining consent in any intimate situation. By setting clear expectations and modeling healthy relationships, parents contribute to the development of healthy sexual attraction in their children.

While parents play a significant role, it is important to recognize that other factors also influence the development of sexual attraction in children. The role of media and technology cannot be underestimated. Exposure to sexual content through various media platforms can shape children's understanding and expectations of relationships and sexuality. It is crucial for parents and educators to monitor and guide children's media consumption to ensure it aligns with their values and promotes healthy sexual development.

Cultural influences also play a role in shaping sexual attraction. Different societies have different norms and values surrounding sexuality, and these can impact children's attitudes and behaviors. Parents and educators can help children navigate cultural influences by providing a safe space for discussion and promoting tolerance and acceptance.

In conclusion, the parent-child bond has long-term effects on the development of sexual attraction in children. By fostering a secure attachment, promoting open communication, and providing guidance, parents can positively influence their children's sexual development. However, it is essential to recognize the impact of other factors such as media, technology, culture, and peer influence. By understanding and addressing these factors, parents and educators can create an environment that supports healthy sexual attraction development in children.

Early Trauma and Adverse Childhood Experiences (ACEs) Impact on Attraction

Early trauma and adverse childhood experiences (ACEs) can have a significant impact on the development of sexual attraction in children. Research has shown that children who experience traumatic events or ACEs may be more susceptible to developing unhealthy or inappropriate sexual attractions later in life.

ACEs, which can include physical, emotional, or sexual abuse, neglect, or witnessing domestic violence, can disrupt a child's sense of safety, trust, and self-worth. These experiences can lead to a range of negative outcomes, including difficulties in forming healthy relationships and a distorted understanding of sexual attraction.

Children who have experienced early trauma may struggle with attachment and trust issues, which can impact their ability to form healthy connections with others. This can manifest in their later sexual attraction, as they may seek out relationships that replicate or reinforce the traumatic experiences they have endured.

Additionally, the psychological and emotional factors associated with ACEs can contribute to the development of inappropriate sexual attraction. Children who have experienced trauma may internalize negative beliefs about themselves or others, leading to distorted perceptions of what is appropriate or healthy in a sexual relationship.

It is important for parents and educators to be aware of the impact of early trauma and ACEs on the development of sexual attraction in children. By providing a safe and supportive environment, adults can help children heal from their past experiences and foster healthy attitudes towards sexuality.

Parental guidance plays a crucial role in shaping a child's understanding of healthy sexual attraction. Open and age-appropriate conversations about relationships, boundaries, consent, and respect can help children develop a healthy framework for their own sexual attraction.

Peer influence also plays a significant role in the development of sexual attraction in children. Educators can create a positive and inclusive classroom environment that promotes healthy relationships and respect for diversity. By teaching children about empathy, communication, and healthy boundaries, educators can empower them to make informed choices regarding their own sexual attraction.

Furthermore, education and awareness programs can play a vital role in promoting healthy sexual attraction development in children. By providing accurate and age-appropriate information about sexuality, these programs can help children develop a positive and healthy understanding of their own sexual attraction.

Intervention strategies are essential for addressing inappropriate sexual attraction in children. Early identification and intervention can prevent the development of harmful behaviors and help children receive the support they need to heal from their traumatic experiences.

In conclusion, early trauma and adverse childhood experiences can have a profound impact on the development of sexual attraction in children. It is crucial for parents and educators to understand the factors shaping sexual attraction in children and to provide the necessary guidance and support to foster healthy attitudes and behaviors. By addressing these issues, we can help children develop positive and healthy relationships throughout their lives.

Chapter 11: Neurological and Hormonal Factors Affecting the Development of Sexual Attraction in Children

Brain Development and the Emergence of Attraction

Understanding the Factors Shaping Sexual Attraction in Children: A Parent's Perspective

Chapter 4: Brain Development and the Emergence of Attraction

As parents and educators, it is essential to understand the intricate factors that shape the development of sexual attraction in children. One crucial aspect to consider is brain development and its impact on the emergence of attraction.

The human brain undergoes significant changes throughout childhood and adolescence, particularly in the areas associated with emotions, decision-making, and social interactions. These changes play a vital role in the development of sexual attraction.

During early childhood, the brain is highly plastic and adaptable, making it susceptible to external influences. Factors such as genetics, early experiences, and environmental stimuli can shape the developing brain and influence the emergence of attraction. This understanding highlights the importance of providing children with a healthy and supportive environment that fosters positive emotional and social development.

Another crucial factor influencing the development of sexual attraction is the role of media and technology. In today's digital age, children are exposed to a vast array of media content that can shape their perceptions of relationships and attractiveness. It is vital for parents and educators to monitor and guide their children's media consumption, promoting positive and age-appropriate content that fosters healthy attitudes towards attraction and relationships.

Cultural influences also significantly impact the development of sexual attraction in children. Different cultures have diverse norms, values, and beliefs surrounding sexuality. Understanding and discussing these cultural influences with children can help them develop a broader perspective and navigate their own emerging attractions in a respectful and inclusive manner.

Parental guidance plays a crucial role in shaping children's understanding and attitudes towards attraction. Open and honest communication about feelings, relationships, and boundaries can help children develop a healthy understanding of attraction from an early age. By providing accurate information and creating a safe space for discussion, parents can empower their children to make informed choices and develop a positive sense of self.

Peer influence is another significant factor in the development of sexual attraction. As children grow older, their interactions with peers become more influential. Educators and parents should encourage healthy peer relationships and provide guidance on setting boundaries and making respectful choices.

Psychological and emotional factors also play a vital role in the development of sexual attraction. Children who have experienced trauma or have emotional challenges may exhibit unique patterns of attraction. It is essential for parents and educators to be aware of these factors and provide appropriate support to help children navigate their feelings.

Education and awareness programs can play a critical role in promoting healthy sexual attraction development in children. By providing age-appropriate information about relationships, consent, and personal boundaries, we can empower children to develop healthy attitudes towards attraction.

Early childhood experiences can have a lasting impact on the development of sexual attraction. Children who have experienced abuse or neglect may require additional support and intervention strategies to address inappropriate or harmful attractions. Identifying and addressing these challenges early on is crucial for the child's well-being and future relationships.

Finally, neurological and hormonal factors also influence the development of sexual attraction in children. Understanding the role of these biological factors can help parents and educators approach attraction development with empathy and compassion.

In conclusion, understanding the factors that shape the development of sexual attraction in children is crucial for parents and educators. By considering brain development, media influences, cultural factors, parental guidance, peer influence, psychological and emotional factors, education programs, early childhood experiences, and biological factors, we can provide the necessary support and guidance to help children navigate their emerging attractions in a healthy and positive way.

Hormonal Changes in Puberty and Their Impact on Sexual Attraction

During puberty, children experience significant hormonal changes that can have a profound impact on their sexual attraction. It is important for parents and educators to understand these changes in order to support children through this stage of development.

Puberty is a period of rapid growth and development, both physically and emotionally. One of the key changes that occur during this time is the activation of the reproductive system, which is regulated by hormones such as estrogen and testosterone. These hormones play a crucial role in the development of secondary sexual characteristics, such as breast development in girls and facial hair growth in boys.

Alongside these physical changes, hormonal fluctuations can also influence sexual attraction. As children enter puberty, they may start to experience feelings of attraction towards others. This is a normal part of their sexual development, and it is important for parents and educators to provide a supportive and non-judgmental environment for children to explore and understand these feelings.

It is worth noting that hormonal changes alone do not determine sexual orientation or attraction. Sexual attraction is a complex interplay of biological, psychological, and social factors. Hormones simply provide a foundation for the development of sexual attraction, but the ultimate expression of this attraction is influenced by a range of other factors.

Understanding the impact of hormonal changes on sexual attraction can help parents and educators navigate conversations about sexuality with children. By acknowledging the biological aspects of sexual attraction, we can provide a more comprehensive understanding of this fundamental aspect of human development.

Additionally, it is important to address any concerns or questions that children may have about their changing bodies and feelings. Open and honest communication is key in supporting children through this phase of their lives. Parents and educators can provide accurate information about puberty and sexual attraction, dispelling any myths or misconceptions that children may have acquired from media or peers.

By understanding the hormonal changes that occur during puberty and their impact on sexual attraction, parents and educators can play a crucial role in guiding children through this transformative stage of their lives.

Understanding the Relationship Between Neurology and Attraction

When it comes to the development of sexual attraction in children, there are various factors at play. One important aspect that should not be overlooked is the connection between neurology and attraction. Neurological and hormonal factors can significantly impact the development of sexual attraction in children, and it is crucial for parents and educators to understand this relationship.

The human brain plays a vital role in shaping sexual attraction. During puberty, the brain undergoes significant changes that affect not only physical growth but also emotional and psychological development. These changes are driven by hormones, such as estrogen and testosterone, which influence the brain's response to sexual stimuli.

Research suggests that certain areas of the brain, such as the amygdala and hypothalamus, are involved in processing sexual attraction. These regions are responsible for regulating emotions, motivation, and sexual behavior. They become more active during puberty, leading to an increased interest in romantic and sexual experiences.

Furthermore, studies have shown that brain chemistry, specifically the levels of neurotransmitters like dopamine and serotonin, can also impact sexual attraction. Dopamine, often referred to as the "pleasure hormone," is released in response to rewarding experiences, including sexual encounters. Serotonin, on the other hand, helps regulate mood and emotions and can influence the intensity of sexual attraction.

Understanding the neurological aspects of sexual attraction in children is crucial for several reasons. Firstly, it helps parents and educators recognize that sexual attraction is a natural part of human development and not something to be ashamed of or ignored. By understanding the biological basis of attraction, adults can provide appropriate guidance and support to children as they navigate their feelings and emotions.

Secondly, the recognition of the neurological underpinnings of attraction can help identify potential issues or challenges that may arise. For example, some children may experience an early onset of sexual attraction or exhibit inappropriate behaviors. In such cases, intervention strategies can be implemented to address these concerns and promote healthy development.

Lastly, knowledge about the neurology of attraction can inform the design of education and awareness programs. By incorporating this understanding into sexual education curricula, educators can provide accurate and age-appropriate information to children, helping them navigate their feelings and make informed choices.

In conclusion, the relationship between neurology and attraction is a crucial aspect of understanding the development of sexual attraction in children. By recognizing the influence of neurological and hormonal factors, parents and educators can better support children as they navigate their feelings and emotions. Additionally, this understanding can inform intervention strategies and education programs, ultimately promoting healthy sexual attraction development in children.

Chapter 12: Intervention Strategies for Addressing Inappropriate Sexual Attraction in Children

Recognizing Red Flags and Warning Signs

In our modern society, the development of sexual attraction in children has become a paramount concern for both parents and educators. As adults responsible for their well-being, it is crucial that we understand the factors shaping this development, as well as the red flags and warning signs to look out for. This subchapter aims to equip you with the knowledge and tools necessary to identify potential issues and take appropriate action.

One of the primary factors influencing the development of sexual attraction in children is the role of media and technology. With easy access to explicit content, children are exposed to sexualized images and messages from a young age. It is essential to be vigilant and monitor their media consumption, as well as engage in open discussions about healthy sexuality.

Cultural influences also play a significant role in shaping sexual attraction. Different cultures have varying beliefs and norms surrounding sexuality, and it is important to be aware of how these influences may impact a child's understanding of their own desires and boundaries.

Parental guidance is crucial in shaping a child's sexual development. By providing accurate and age-appropriate information, parents can foster a healthy understanding of sexuality. Additionally, parents should be attuned to any changes in behavior or signs of distress that may indicate an issue with sexual attraction.

Peer influence is another factor that can significantly impact a child's sexual attraction. As children grow older, their friends become an essential part of their lives. It is essential to promote positive peer relationships and educate children about consent and boundaries.

Psychological and emotional factors also play a role in shaping sexual attraction. Traumatic experiences or emotional disturbances can influence a child's understanding of sexuality. Recognizing these factors and seeking appropriate professional help is crucial to ensure a child's well-being.

Education and awareness programs are vital in promoting healthy sexual attraction development. By implementing comprehensive sex education in schools and providing resources for parents, children can learn about consent, boundaries, and healthy relationships from an early age.

Early childhood experiences, including abuse or neglect, can have a profound impact on a child's sexual development. Recognizing the signs of trauma and providing appropriate support is essential to help children heal and develop healthy attitudes towards sexuality.

Neurological and hormonal factors also influence the development of sexual attraction. Understanding the biological aspects of sexual development can help parents and educators better comprehend the challenges children may face.

Finally, intervention strategies for addressing inappropriate sexual attraction are crucial. It is essential to create a safe space for children to express their concerns and seek help when needed. Professionals specializing in child psychology and sexual development can offer guidance and support in these situations.

In conclusion, recognizing red flags and warning signs in the development of sexual attraction in children is of utmost importance for parents and educators. By understanding the various factors that shape this development, we can take proactive steps to promote healthy attitudes towards sexuality and intervene when necessary.

Seeking Professional Help and Guidance

When it comes to the development of sexual attraction in children, it is crucial for parents and educators to be well-informed and equipped with the right tools to address this sensitive topic. While it is normal for children to experience curiosity and questions about their bodies and the opposite sex, there are instances where seeking professional help and guidance becomes necessary.

Factors influencing the development of sexual attraction in children are complex and multifaceted. The role of media and technology cannot be underestimated, as it exposes children to sexual content at an earlier age than ever before. Additionally, cultural influences play a significant role in shaping children's understanding of sexuality. These factors can have both positive and negative effects, highlighting the importance of guidance from professionals who can help navigate these influences.

Parental guidance is a key factor in the development of sexual attraction in children. Open and honest communication between parents and their children can create a safe space for discussions about sexuality. Parents who are informed and comfortable discussing these topics can have a positive impact on their children's understanding and development of healthy sexual attraction.

Peer influence is another important aspect to consider. Children often look to their peers for guidance, and their attitudes and behaviors can influence their understanding of sexuality. Professionals can help parents and educators understand how to address peer influence and guide children towards healthy sexual development.

Psychological and emotional factors can also influence sexual attraction in children. Traumatic experiences, such as abuse or neglect, can have a lasting impact on a child's understanding of sexuality. Seeking professional help can provide strategies to address these issues and help children develop a healthy understanding of their own bodies and relationships.

Education and awareness programs play a crucial role in promoting healthy sexual attraction development in children. Professionals can guide parents and educators on age-appropriate resources and strategies to educate children about consent, boundaries, and healthy relationships.

Early childhood experiences can have a lasting impact on the development of sexual attraction. Professionals can help parents and educators understand the potential effects of these experiences and provide intervention strategies to address any negative impacts.

Finally, neurological and hormonal factors can affect the development of sexual attraction in children. Seeking professional help can provide a better understanding of these factors and how they may influence a child's behavior and development.

In conclusion, seeking professional help and guidance is essential for parents and educators when addressing the development of sexual attraction in children. Professionals can provide valuable insights, strategies, and resources to navigate the many factors that influence children's understanding of sexuality. By working together, we can create a safe and healthy environment for children to develop a positive and informed understanding of their own bodies and relationships.

Creating a Supportive Environment for Recovery and Healing

In this subchapter, we will explore the importance of creating a supportive environment for children's recovery and healing from inappropriate sexual attraction. As parents and educators, it is crucial for us to understand the factors that shape sexual attraction in children and how we can play a role in fostering a healthy development.

One of the key factors influencing the development of sexual attraction in children is the role of media and technology. In today's digital age, children are exposed to various forms of media that can impact their understanding of sexuality. It is essential for parents and educators to monitor and regulate their children's media consumption, ensuring that they are exposed to age-appropriate content.

Cultural influences also play a significant role in the development of sexual attraction in children. Different cultures have different norms and values regarding sexuality, and it is important to provide children with a comprehensive understanding of diverse perspectives. By promoting open and honest discussions about sexuality, we can help children develop a healthy and inclusive view of relationships and attraction.

Parental guidance is another crucial factor in shaping children's sexual attraction development. Parents should maintain open lines of communication with their children, providing accurate information about sexuality and addressing any concerns or questions they may have. By creating a safe and non-judgmental space, parents can support their children's emotional well-being and help them navigate through any challenges they may face.

Peer influence also plays a significant role in the development of sexual attraction in children. As parents and educators, we should encourage positive peer relationships and provide guidance on healthy boundaries and respectful behavior. By fostering a supportive social environment, we can help children develop healthy relationships and reduce the likelihood of inappropriate sexual attraction.

Psychological and emotional factors can also influence children's sexual attraction development. Traumatic experiences or adverse childhood events may affect their understanding of relationships and attraction. It is important to provide appropriate therapy and counseling to children who have experienced such events, ensuring their emotional well-being and supporting their recovery process.

Furthermore, education and awareness programs can play a critical role in promoting healthy sexual attraction development in children. By incorporating comprehensive sexual education in schools and communities, we can equip children with the necessary knowledge and skills to navigate their own sexuality confidently.

Early childhood experiences, neurological, and hormonal factors also impact the development of sexual attraction in children. Understanding these influences can help parents and educators identify potential red flags and seek appropriate intervention strategies when necessary. Early intervention can significantly contribute to addressing inappropriate sexual attraction and supporting a child's recovery and healing process.

In conclusion, creating a supportive environment for recovery and healing is vital for children's healthy sexual attraction development. By understanding the various factors that shape sexual attraction in children and implementing appropriate strategies, parents and educators can play a crucial role in supporting children's well-being and helping them navigate their sexuality with confidence.

Chapter 13: Conclusion

Summarizing Key Findings and Insights

In the subchapter titled "Summarizing Key Findings and Insights," we will provide a comprehensive overview of the various factors that shape sexual attraction in children, aimed at parents and educators. By understanding these factors, we can effectively support healthy sexual development in children and address any potential concerns.

Throughout our exploration of the development of sexual attraction in children, we have identified several key findings. Firstly, we have observed that various factors influence the development of sexual attraction in children. These include biological, psychological, and social factors, all of which interact to shape a child's understanding of their own sexuality.

One significant factor that cannot be overlooked is the role of media and technology in shaping sexual attraction in children. Exposure to explicit content, inappropriate advertisements, and online interactions can impact a child's perception of sexuality. It is essential for parents and educators to be vigilant and establish guidelines to ensure age-appropriate media consumption.

Cultural influences also play a crucial role in shaping sexual attraction in children. Cultural norms, beliefs, and values can impact a child's understanding of sexuality and influence their behavior. Therefore, it is important to promote open and inclusive discussions around sexuality, respecting diverse perspectives and fostering acceptance.

Parental guidance is another influential factor in the development of sexual attraction. Parents must provide accurate information, create a safe environment for open dialogue, and be proactive in discussing healthy relationships and boundaries. By doing so, parents can positively impact their child's sexual development.

Peer influence is another aspect to consider. Children often learn from their peers, and it is important to educate them about healthy relationships and consent to counter any negative influences they may encounter.

Psychological and emotional factors also play a significant role in a child's sexual development. Traumatic experiences, self-esteem issues, or emotional instability can impact a child's understanding of sexuality. Therefore, it is crucial to address any underlying psychological or emotional concerns through therapy or counseling.

Education and awareness programs are vital for promoting healthy sexual development in children. Providing age-appropriate information, teaching consent, and promoting healthy relationships through school-based programs can empower children with the knowledge and skills they need to navigate their sexual development.

Early childhood experiences, neurological, and hormonal factors also affect a child's sexual attraction. By understanding these factors, parents and educators can better support children who may be experiencing atypical or inappropriate sexual attraction.

Finally, we explore intervention strategies for addressing inappropriate sexual attraction in children. Early identification, seeking professional help, and implementing appropriate therapy or counseling can ensure that children receive the support they need.

In conclusion, understanding the factors shaping sexual attraction in children is crucial for parents and educators. By summarizing the key findings and insights presented in this subchapter, we aim to equip our audience with the knowledge and tools necessary to support healthy sexual development in children and address any potential concerns effectively.

Empowering Parents and Educators to Foster Healthy Sexual Attraction Development

In today's society, it is imperative for parents and educators to understand the factors shaping sexual attraction in children. The development of sexual attraction is a natural part of growing up, and it is crucial that we provide the necessary guidance and support to ensure it develops in a healthy and positive manner.

One of the key factors influencing the development of sexual attraction in children is the role of media and technology. With the proliferation of smartphones, social media, and online content, children are exposed to a wide range of sexualized images and messages at an early age. Parents and educators need to be aware of the impact this exposure can have and take steps to monitor and limit their child's media consumption.

Cultural influences also play a significant role in the development of sexual attraction in children. Different cultures have different norms and values surrounding sexuality, and it is important for parents and educators to be sensitive to these cultural differences. By understanding and embracing diversity, we can create an environment that fosters healthy sexual attraction development.

Parental guidance is paramount in shaping a child's understanding of sexual attraction. Open and honest communication between parents and children is essential. Parents should provide age-appropriate information about sexuality and answer any questions their child may have. By creating a safe space for discussion, parents can help their child navigate the complexities of sexual attraction.

Peer influence is another factor that cannot be overlooked. Children often look to their peers for guidance and validation, and it is crucial for parents and educators to promote positive peer relationships. Encouraging healthy friendships and teaching children to respect boundaries will help them develop a healthy understanding of sexual attraction.

Psychological and emotional factors also play a significant role in shaping sexual attraction in children. Traumatic experiences or unresolved emotional issues can impact a child's development in this area. Recognizing the signs of distress and providing appropriate support and counseling can help children overcome these challenges.

Education and awareness programs are essential in promoting healthy sexual attraction development. Schools and community organizations should provide age-appropriate sex education that focuses on consent, healthy relationships, and respect. By equipping children with the knowledge and skills they need, we can empower them to make informed decisions about their own bodies and relationships.

Early childhood experiences have a profound impact on the development of sexual attraction. Positive and nurturing environments can lay the foundation for healthy relationships later in life. Parents and educators should strive to create a supportive and loving atmosphere, where children feel safe to explore and ask questions.

Neurological and hormonal factors also influence the development of sexual attraction in children. Understanding the biological aspects of puberty and sexual development can help parents and educators support children through this transformative stage.

Lastly, intervention strategies are necessary for addressing inappropriate sexual attraction in children. If a child exhibits concerning behaviors or displays a lack of understanding about appropriate boundaries, it is crucial to seek professional help. Early intervention can prevent further harm and ensure the child receives the support they need.

In conclusion, empowering parents and educators to foster healthy sexual attraction development in children is a vital responsibility. By understanding the various factors that shape sexual attraction and implementing appropriate strategies, we can create a safe and supportive environment for children to navigate this aspect of their lives.

Looking Towards the Future: Promoting Positive Change in Society's Understanding of Childhood Attraction.

Looking Towards the Future: Promoting Positive Change in Society's Understanding of Childhood Attraction

As parents and educators, it is our responsibility to understand and address the factors shaping sexual attraction in children. By gaining a deeper understanding of this complex topic, we can support healthy development and guide children towards appropriate behaviors. In this subchapter, we will explore the various aspects that influence the development of sexual attraction in children and discuss the role each of us plays in promoting positive change.

One crucial factor that cannot be ignored is the impact of media and technology on children's understanding of attraction. With the rise of digital platforms, children are exposed to a vast range of content, some of which may be inappropriate for their age. It is our duty to monitor and guide their media consumption, ensuring that they receive appropriate information and messages about relationships and consent.

Cultural influences also play a significant role in shaping children's understanding of attraction. Different societies have varying norms and values, and it is essential to acknowledge and challenge any harmful beliefs or stereotypes that may perpetuate unhealthy attitudes towards sexuality. By fostering open and inclusive discussions, we can help children develop a healthy understanding of attraction that respects diversity.

Parental guidance is paramount in the development of children's sexual attraction. By providing accurate and age-appropriate information, parents can demystify the topic and create a safe space for open dialogue. Parents should also be aware of the impact of their own behaviors and attitudes, as children often model their understanding of attraction based on their parents' example.

Peer influence is another crucial aspect to consider. Children are highly influenced by their friends and may adopt certain attitudes or behaviors. It is crucial for parents and educators to foster a supportive environment where healthy relationships and boundaries are encouraged.

Psychological and emotional factors cannot be overlooked, as they greatly influence children's understanding of attraction. By addressing emotions, building self-esteem, and teaching empathy, we can help children develop healthy relationships and navigate their feelings appropriately.

Education and awareness programs are powerful tools in shaping healthy sexual attraction development in children. By implementing comprehensive sex education programs in schools and providing resources for parents, we can equip children with the knowledge and skills they need to make informed decisions and develop positive attitudes towards relationships.

Early childhood experiences and neurological and hormonal factors also contribute to the development of sexual attraction in children.

Understanding these influences can help us identify potential red flags and intervene early if necessary.

Finally, we must address inappropriate sexual attraction in children by implementing effective intervention strategies. This may involve seeking professional help, providing therapy, and creating a supportive environment for the child to heal and learn appropriate behaviors.

In conclusion, by understanding the various factors shaping sexual attraction in children, we can promote positive change in society's understanding of this complex topic. Through parental guidance, education, and awareness programs, we can foster healthy development and equip children with the tools they need to navigate their feelings and relationships in a positive and respectful manner. Together, we can create a future where children grow up with a healthy understanding of attraction and consent.